Irineu Ruzza Romanato

Smart Concepts

Do you think that you need it?

"Persistence is the companion of excellence; embrace methodology as your guide and turn every challenge into a ladder to your success."

Unknown Author

Dedication

First of all, I would like to dedicate this book to several people that was and are very important in my life, my special thanks to all.

I would like to first thanks to God, the Great Light that controls and architects my life and who has always been guiding my steps.

My beloved mother who has always been my safe haven and my loved brother (Tato) who has been showing me at all the time how to be the Man I am today. He is one of the marvelous angels that God send to our lives to complete the spaces that nobody can fill and making our lives better. I really love you my brother.

Two special people that arrives in my live and makes me a better person. My children's, Victor and Leticia, who are the most important light of my life. They are the greatest gift I could have gotten from God.
My loved wife who has a monstrous patience to endure my moments of absence while I'm working a lot, writing this book or teaching in my class.

The special thanks to my grandparents (Ellen and Seraphin) who have been, are and always will be my eternal stars that shine in my starry sky and show the way I should go, they are the stars that I seek in the sky when I realize that I am feeling lost.

To my special 3 friends that I keep in my heart for over 35 years, and they never ceased to encourage my literary, professional and personal adventures, Mario Nelson, affectionately called by my children's of "Tio Mario", Ricardo that my children loved and affectionately call "Tio Pasqua", these guys are completely part of my life.
I reserved a special space to dedicate my book and say a special thanks to another very special friend that unfortunately my children did not have the opportunity and honor to know. I would like to thank you very much for the years that he was with us in this physical plane, my eternal friend and brother Renato ("metal"), we will see each other, my dear, and that hug that was missed I'll give to you.

Thank you all!!

I.   Summary

1. Preface

From the oldest armies and empires to the most advanced hospitals and schools today, there have always been words that sounded like mantras for the success of these institutions.

Scientists, philosophers, thinkers or geniuses who lived with us made their discoveries, wrote their treatises or philosophies enjoying moments of nature and human behavior, finding in this momentum the same word that as a mantra always brought success when used correctly;

"Standard or Standardization"

Have you allowed yourself a few minutes to look at the world around you and thereby capture the behaviors and patterns of all things and creatures that surround you?

I invite you to do so, the experience will be fascinating.

A company or person that denies the exaggerated pursuit of standards, procedures, and documentation of existing processes will not have the privilege of celebrating many birthdays.

When I show to my students the methodologies for pattern analysis I really like to start by showing a hummingbird's flight, which sacredly follows certain patterns, soon after I go to medieval documents or treatises like "The Prince of Machiavelli" or older documents more effective as "Sun Tzu - The Art of War", and soon after I return to today's standards used by NASA to correct flight time faults, those we see in movies and see someone open a manual and start following step by step from the simplest and most mundane to the most complex failure to analyze often has strong motivations; means everyone's life and the tools to correct problems are restricted. Be your best in this moment.

In all the cases above the detailed analysis shows that everything should always be analyzed, documented and especially following a pattern, if there was a certain failure some point should be re-analyzed to find the lack of standard and or standardization, in short, the non-respect to an implemented procedure.

Whenever an empire or large organization sought to equalize all its points through procedures and based it on standards, success was certain.

The similarity of patterns implemented in production environments in the era of Henry Ford or pattern analysis done by Renè Descartes to arrive at his discoveries and even similarities or patterns analyzed by Einstein and Marie Curie were as the keys to the evolution of humanity. Following from basic like the atomic analysis or complex mathematical algorithms that today underlie the evolution of quantum computing and artificial intelligence.

Soon we will have computers analyzing human behavior and nature behavior in real time and with the help of artificial intelligence, machine learning and complex decision-making algorithms, we will make a difference in our evolution and this will be technological milestones.

Some will say that this will also bring us the complex abstraction of human relations, that is already happening in my opinion, but let's leave this theme for another book.

Welcome aboard and let's have fun together on this adventure by discovering how to implement technology standards.

2. How to use this book

In this book there was never a pretense to make a manual on ITIL and its principles, we understand that professionals who seek this literature are already used to the standards and actually seek a guide on how to facilitate its implementation.

This book is divided in some topics that make easy the way that must be followed. In the first moment we are talking about monitoring the environment, incident management and after talk about change management process.

Let's Start this journey!!!
Be my guest….

3. Introduction

As an IT professional for many years, I have always faced one big problem and believe many other faced as well.

The need to implement small day-to-day controls routines in the technology area without a guideline to start and make sure that are in the right way.

After the compilation of ITIL and COBIT I realized that our life in IT going to be easier, but then soon the big questions came up;

- "How should I start ???"
- "How to fit this process to our company size???"
- "Is it mandatory to use all the point of the procedure?"

This question with absolute certainty has taken the sleep of many technology professionals in recent years and even nowadays it still does, because often the budget is short and deadlines even more, without the challenge of implementing something and creating the culture within of an organization and there begins the great challenges.

Over the past few year's countless corporations, and when I say countless talk about values over 50, have had serious problems in their production, development, or testing environments due to total lack of control over changes in their technology environments.

The major part of this issues stopped the production environment for more the 2 days and highly impact in the company financial stocks or money.

The arrival of large cloud providers and the ease of changing entire environments with few clicks and lots of money has turned managers' dreams into despair.

I am a professional that born in technology environments in the old way, with mainframes and an absurd control of everything that was being done, what would still be done and even what we once thought to do, because the costs and criticism of the environments and processes were brought to a level of control that approached NASA environments.

Right after the advent of virtualization for midsize servers, the ease of having development and test environments that would come very close to production environments was the first dream come true.

Now with the advent of cloud the ease for everything is simply monstrous and there is no limit, well there is actually how much money you can spend.

4. Agile Challenge

When the fever of Agile implementations began, I remember well that many professionals gave the death sentence to the entire ITIL process, as for some with misunderstanding about Agile the two processes could never live in the same environment.
At the first opportunity I had with one of these professionals I tried to understand the reasons he had for this sad death sentence.
It was at this point that I understood and was absolutely certain that this misunderstanding of technologies would make all ITIL standards an even more important and irreplaceable set of rules.
Today I can say that YES, the two standards can and should live in the same environment and one must complement the other, as IILE-associated AGILE

development make a mature technology environment more dynamic and mostly safer and more controlled.

Let's talk about this mature coexistence in the next topics.

5. Cloud Environment

Azure, Amazon and Google, not to mention other less significant providers at the moment in the cloud offering market, are the countless alternatives for all technology managers to make big changes, dust off their racks and start shifting their physical environments to virtual environments relying on virtual reality. previously unimaginable redundancies, geo-replication and especially advanced features that are available in 2 or 3 clicks and allow for a secure, stable and controlled environment, but all have a financial cost coming from the other side of the scale showing that if you can now implement a Two or three click load balancers will also spend a significant amount and all of this should be checked day by day.

6. How to control de costs?

The costs will be every-day-problem and the only way to control and mitigate the expenses will be a simple word that returning you back (you means managers) many and many years ago, like was in the mainframe time.

CONTROL!!!
Lot of Controls and procedures

The environment must be controlled not only for access or security but when we talk about changes, change can affect financial points and other topics when its failure and created an incident for example.

In this book we will talk about some controls that makes the way easier to create and implement simple rules that helps the managers to watch the environment using a more controlled eye.

7. Monitoring Management

7.1. Talking about the monitoring

Monitoring management is a concept that enables an organization to maximize business value from the use of information technology.

An entire monitoring process helps the organization to prevent problems with your systems or environments, to be more proactive or have a more proactive image according to the customer perspective, and then give to the customer a better experience and availability.

This small groups of opportunities brings to the company when literally translate, money or revenues.

Every moment that the technology environment is stopped the customer start to have a worst experience and start to think about your competitors.

A lot of business studies was made in the last year that show the customer behavior and one of more damage behaviors only appear when they face problems with IT contracts.

Let's start our journey to describe how to create a monitoring environment from the scratch and improve the company and customer experience.

7.2. Audience

This document has been created for computer monitoring teams, system and network administrators, security staff, technical support staff, chief information security officers (CISOs), chief information officers (CIOs), computer security program managers, and others who are responsible for preparing for, or responding to, security incidents.

7.3. The monitoring processes.

Monitoring process is a group of actions and process that result in a creation of area and can be translated in a group of people working with an effort to look the entire environment and trying to identify possible problems, abnormal behaviors in all the technology areas and mainly execute some actions when discover a problem.

As a sample of this actions, the monitoring team can pull the trigger to have all the incident team ready to act in an incident or the change management committee to prepare a solution or correction to an environment that indicated an issue or abnormal behavior.

In the topics below we will explain better how to compose the monitor area and how to compose the team in this area, but be aware that the core of all the monitoring area is the service catalog and responsibility matrix that we will talk about in the next topics.

7.4. Categorization of Monitoring

The title for this topic is a terrible point because during the monitoring process the team must to monitoring the whole environment without discrimination, but unfortunately this is not the true.

When you create a service catalog one of the important point in the document is a categorization of the service and a prioritization of the service according the criticality.

In this document we will work with a small division or categorization to guarantee a basic understanding.

We can divide an environment in 4 categories according to the list below;

- infrastructure
- telecommunication
- security
- system or applications

7.5. Categories

Below we discuss about each category and tell about the concept of each one, but the most important point to understand is the flexibility to create more categories when you want but no more than you can manager or classify.

A good exercise to do in this case is a brainstorm with the areas involved in the monitoring process creation to verify, according to the asset list that you have, the real accommodation of the assets or resources or applications inside of the categories.

Talking about an experience, I personally saw more 2 or 3 categories in the list when the company split the telecommunication in 2 categories for call center and applications in 2 categories when they split application internal and external like clouded hosted.

Let's explore some information's below;

1. Infrastructure

In this category normally, we assigned all the assets or resources that compose the basic structure of the technology area.

Normally in this topic we insert computer, server, departmental network devices, virtualization resources, printers, temperature control, surveillance cameras and some access control devices or biometric device used in the entire company.

2. Telecommunication

Telecom are a very wide item and can support a huge list of items that must be monitored. In my opinion this category is a very big challenge.

Following some examples in this category core network devices that control the entire network, critical and redundant links that's provide internet, voice or critical connectivity, corporative PBX and Callcenter resources normally are under this topic.

3. Security

Security is easy to classify when you use a simple rule and question;

"Is this item a protection, security barrier or a device that bring security to the environment?"

Following the question above will be easy to classify the asset, but under this topic normally are inserted firewall, proxies, WAF, antispam and other appliances that make a barrier.

4. System or Applications

I use one rule to this item that helps a lot. All the items that remain in the list without a classification or items that are accessible by customer stay in this category.

Some examples can be CRM, ERP, Financial, expense control, corporative website, HR system and others applications.

7.6. Prioritization

According the 4 categories below you can classify the priority of the monitoring and involve the right team or handling correctly.

Normally the solution or software's that monitoring the environment according to the threshold configured show the prioritization or criticality in different colors, like.

- green or blue means the object or resource are stable, up and running.

- or means the object or resource are stable but running with some different behavior or over the threshold.

- red means the object or resource are stable but running over the capacity.

- **dark** means the object or resource can be reachable or are not running.

Category	Description
Critical (C) **dark**	• Environment are completely affected, and business impact are immediate
High (H) red	• The damage caused by the Incident increases rapidly. • A minor Incident can be prevented from becoming a major Incident by acting immediately. • Several users with VIP status are affected.
Medium (M) **or**	• The damage caused by the Incident increases considerably over time. • A single user with VIP status is affected.
Low (L) green **or** blue	• The damage caused by the Incident only marginally increases over time.

7.7. Business Impact

According to the criticality of the incident the team will involve more or less people, put more or less focus and sometimes declare a situation that's need a war room to solve the problem. Another topic about war room will be in other topics.

Category	Description
Critical (c)	<ul><li>Business impact is immediate</li><li>Revenues impacts are high.</li></ul>
High (H)	<ul><li>A large number of staff are affected and/or not able to do their job.</li><li>A large number of customers are affected and/or acutely disadvantaged in some way.</li><li>The financial impact of the Incident is (for example) likely to exceed $10,000.</li><li>The damage to the reputation of the business is likely to be high.</li><li>Someone has been injured.</li></ul>
Medium (M)	<ul><li>A moderate number of staff are affected and/or not able to do their job properly.</li><li>A moderate number of customers are affected and/or inconvenienced in some way.</li><li>The financial impact of the Incident is (for example) likely to exceed $1,000 but will not be more than $10,000.</li><li>The damage to the reputation of the business is likely to be moderate.</li></ul>
Low (L)	<ul><li>A minimal number of staff are affected and/or able to deliver an acceptable service but this requires extra effort.</li><li>A minimal number of customers are affected and/or inconvenienced but not in a significant way.</li><li>The financial impact of the Incident is (for example) likely to be less than $1,000.</li><li>The damage to the reputation of the business is likely to be minimal.</li></ul>

7.8. Incident Priority Matrix

If classes are defined to rate urgency and impact (see above), an Urgency-Impact Matrix (also referred to as Incident Priority Matrix) can be used to define priority classes, identified in this example by colors and priority codes:

Level		Impact		
		H	M	N
	H	1	2	3
Critical	M	2	3	4
	L	3	4	5

7.9. Resolution time

According to the table below you can find the time to solve each critical incident that's follow the same priority list that's used in Incident Management, because the two areas are completed connected and involved.

Priority Code	Description	Target Response Time	Target Resolution Time
1	Critical	Immediate	1 Hour
2	High	10 Minutes	4 Hours
3	Medium	1 Hour	8 Hours
4	Low	4 Hours	24 Hours
5	Very low	1 Day	1 Week

8. Support Documentation

8.1. Service Catalog

Is a simple list, but extremally important, that are composed by all the services or software or applications that are in the inside of the monitoring process, be monitored.

This list normally has the product, criticality, person responsible and other information's that compose the catalog.

One of the most important pieces of information that rest in the service catalog is the service/application behavior or threshold. Normally this file is used by the monitoring team to build the dashboard and configure the triggers about each application behavior and each trigger that be pulled for each event.

8.2. Responsibility Matrix

This file consolidated all the information's about the service and all the people involved in the process to care the service, some companies compile the service catalog and responsibility matrix in the same file split in two folders.

The matrix indicated who is the people that are responsible for each aspect of the application and how to reach this person, with this information the support team, incident team or monitoring team normally reach the right person in the right time.

As an advice this file must be created for the 3 process, incident management, change management process and monitoring process.

9. Monitoring Management

Let's compose the monitoring area and create the monitoring team with all the resource necessaries to do the actions.

This topic is divided in 3 topics that's explain about people to compose the team, logical access to reach the applications, physical resources to accommodate the team.

9.1. People

A basic list of people as a resource can be describe, but the size of the environment directly affects the quantity of people.

Follow the list below and find some important resources that can vary or not.

Position	Qtd	Description
Monitor Manager	1	For entire area
Shift Coordinator	1	For every work shift
Analysts	2	At least - every work shift

9.2. Logical Access

The people in the monitoring area must have access to all the environments that are in the company, the list below can better help.

Logical Access	Description
Internet Access	Controlled, monitored but unrestricted
Internal network access	Controlled, monitored
Intranet or Knowledge base	Controlled, monitored
Access to the team	Unrestricted
A replica of all the documentation and procedure	Local, controlled and verified every time.

9.3. Physical resources

A list of physical resource can vary depends of the size of the team and work shifts that you need.

Physical Resources	Description
Room	
Computers and Big Monitors	
TVs to be the dashboards	
Small room to be the war room	
Flipcharts and whiteboards	
Celular or PBX Lines	

10. Papers and Responsibility

10.1. Monitor Manager

The Monitor Manager is the person or figure responsible for whole monitoring team and actions and all the critical decisions must be taken from him.

He is the person that make a bridge between the monitoring team and the other areas. In case of a disaster recovery or critical incident he will be the first person to pull the trigger and insert the other managers to start the committee for crisis, like incident, change or disaster recovery.

10.2. Coordinator

Person responsible to coordinate the analysts, produce reports, consolidate the number and give all the information's to the monitor manager. In an event of crisis, he stays inside of the monitoring area given outputs to the manager that are in the committee.

The coordinator is responsible to trainee the new analysts and verify with involved areas if the procedures are updated or changes (RFC) was approved and when they will be executed. As part of your job he keeps the analysts updated about every event that can affected the monitoring.

10.3. Analysts

Technicians trained to look the dashboards and verify each alarm or environment behavior to identify an issue. The contact with the 1st level support team normally are done by the analysts that analyze the problem, verify in the documentation and in the changes (RFC) that are programmed to be executed if the alarm is a positive, false positive or other behavior.

11. Monitoring Management Process

11.1. Monitoring Life Cycle Diagram

The image below shows a workflow process about the life cycle of monitoring process and the interaction with the Incident Response team.

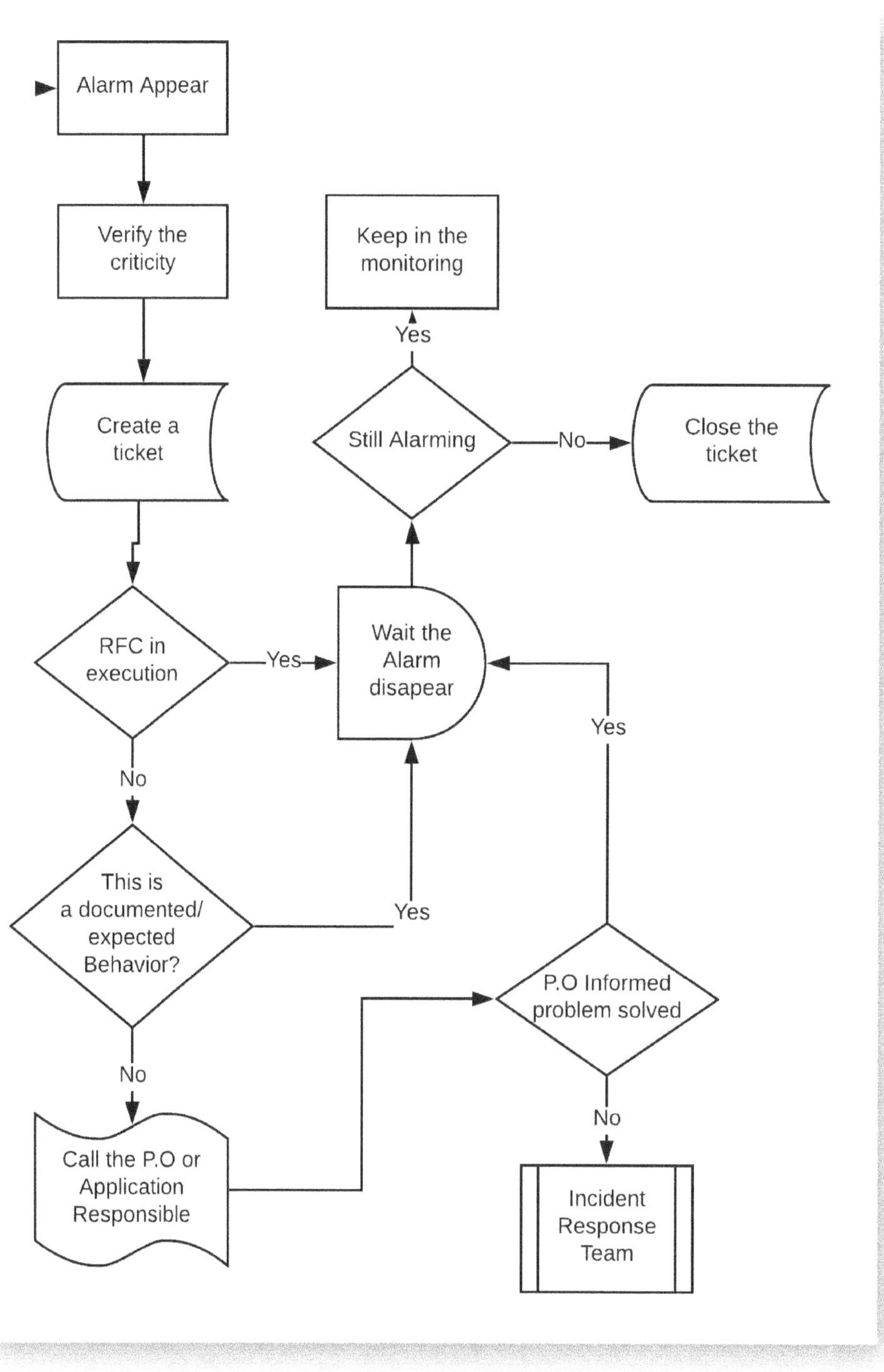

11.2. Monitoring Steps

Below follow the steps used to monitoring according to the diagram above and following the steps that the ITIL standard informed to be followed.

- Monitoring team receive an alarm in the dashboard.
- According to the service catalog, verify the criticality.
- Open a ticket in the internal system.
- Verify in the RFC list, if there are RFC in execution.
  - If yes wait the alarm to disappear
  - If the alarm disappears close the ticket
- Verify if the behavior is expected.
  - If yes wait the alarm to disappear
  - If No verify in the Responsibility Matrix and call the responsible person.
- If the P.O solve the problem, inform to close the ticket when the alarm disappears.
- If the problem is more complex the P.O invoke the Incident team.

12. Model Forms

12.1. Monitoring Lifecycle Diagram

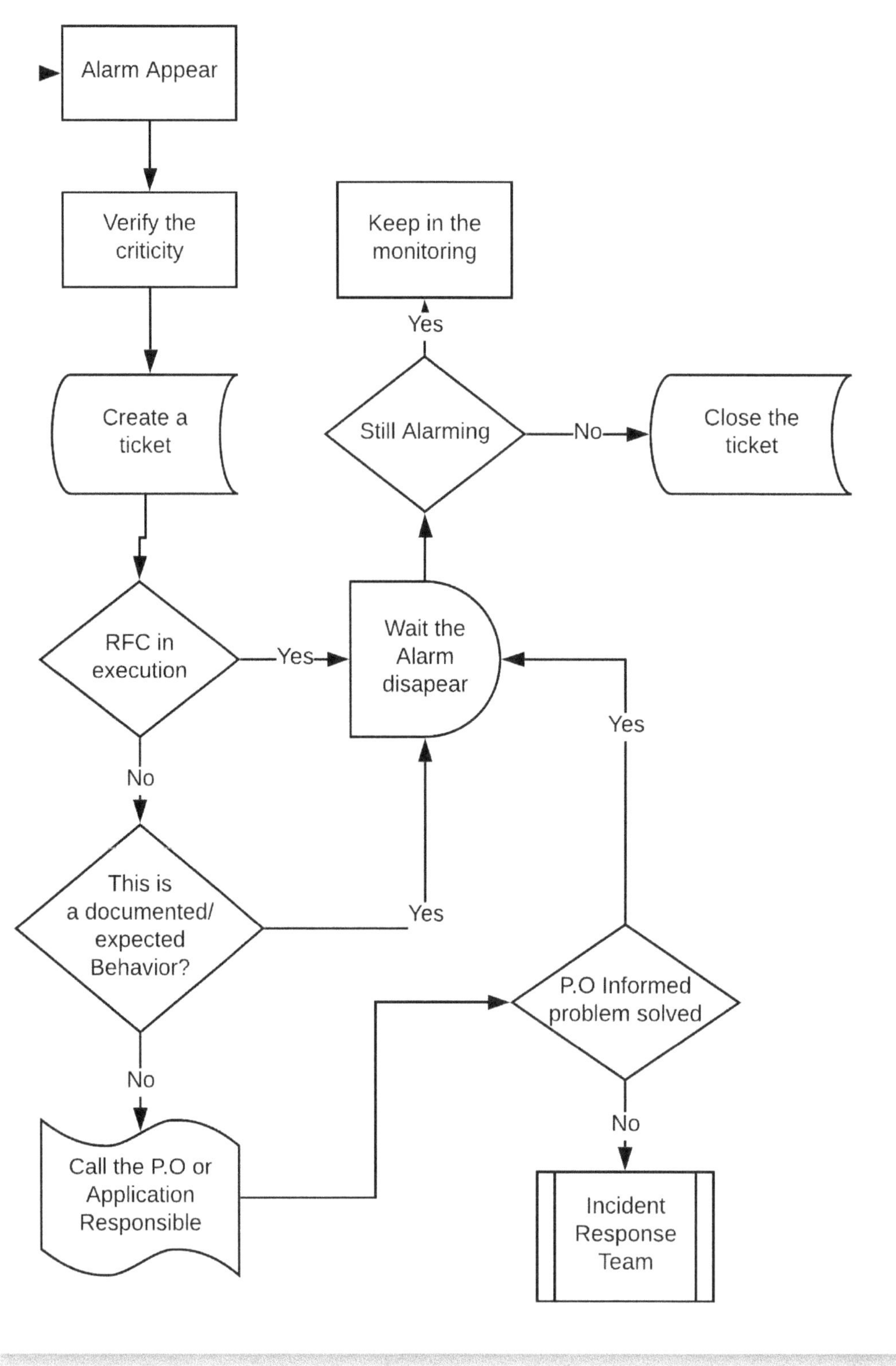

12.2. Responsibility Matrix

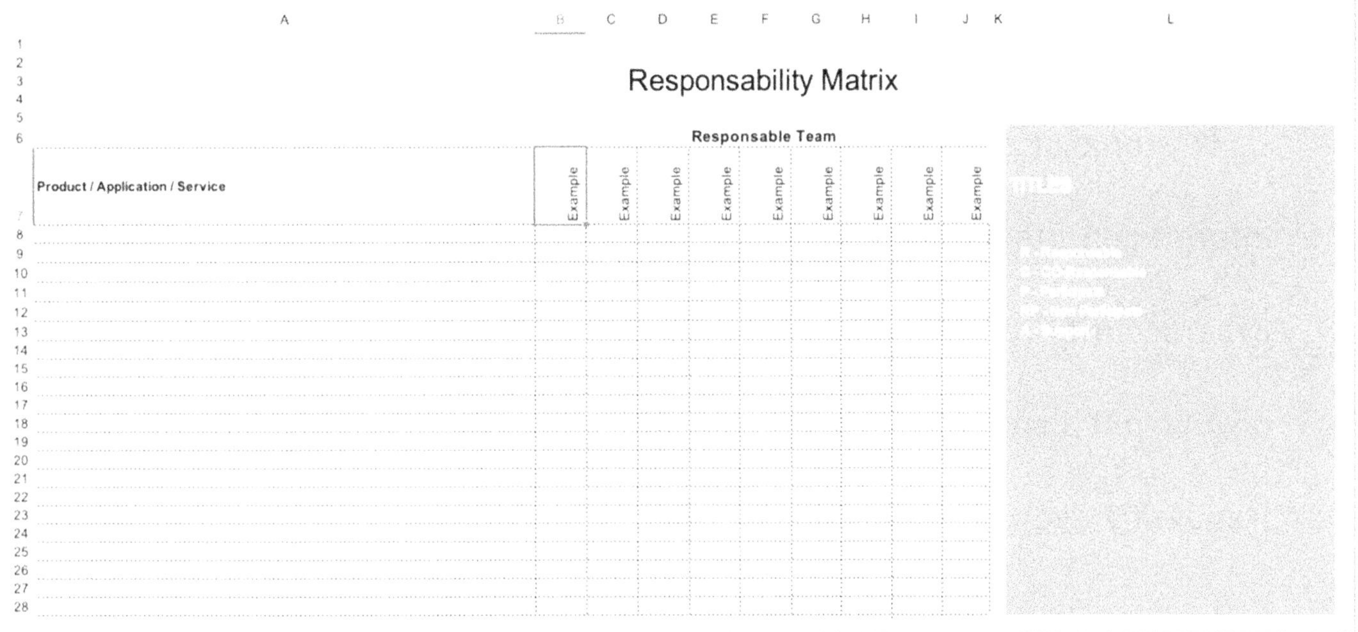

12.3. Service Catalog

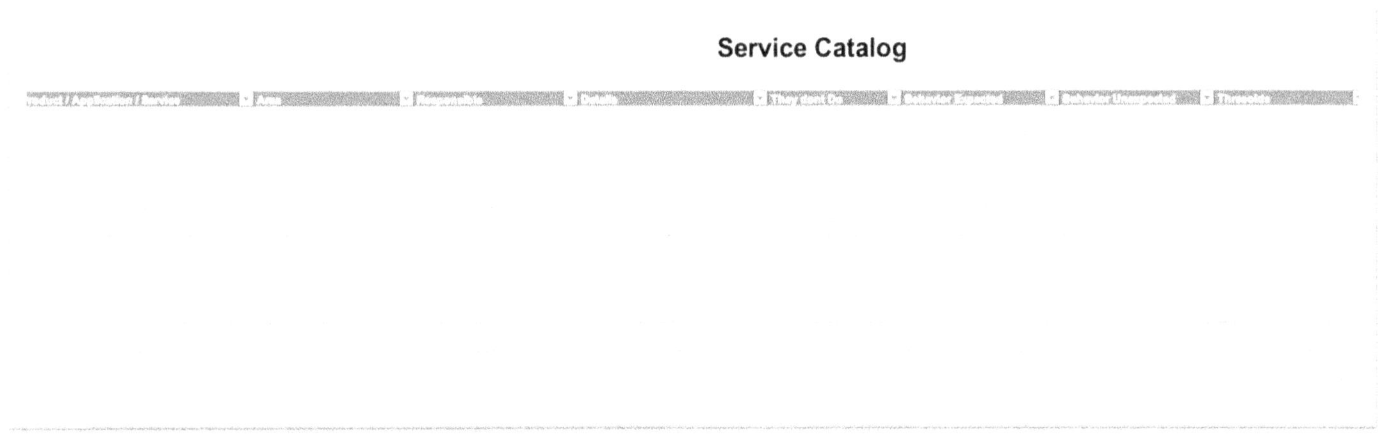

13. Incident Management

13.1. Presentation

Technologic incident response has become an important component of information technology (IT) programs. Operations process failure or cybersecurity-related attacks have become not only more numerous and diverse but also more damaging and disruptive. New types of incidents emerge frequently even security-related. Preventive activities based on the results of risk assessments can lower the number of incidents, but not all incidents can be prevented. An incident response capability is therefore necessary for rapidly detecting incidents, minimizing loss and destruction, mitigating the weaknesses that were exploited, and restoring technologic services.

To that end, this document provides guidelines for incident handling, particularly for analyzing incident-related data and determining the appropriate response to each incident. The guidelines can be followed independently of particular hardware platforms, operating systems, protocols, or applications.

Because performing incident response effectively is a complex undertaking, establishing a successful incident response capability requires substantial planning and resources. Continually monitoring for attacks is essential. Establishing clear procedures for prioritizing the handling of incidents is critical, as is implementing effective methods of collecting, analyzing, and reporting data. It is also vital to build relationships and establish suitable means of communication with other internal groups (e.g., human resources, legal) and with external groups (e.g., other incident response teams, law enforcement).

This publication assists organizations in establishing computer incident and security incidents response capabilities and handling incidents efficiently and effectively.

Understanding threats and identifying modern attacks or bad behaviors in their early stages is key to preventing subsequent compromises, and proactively sharing information among organizations regarding the signs of these attacks is an increasingly effective way to identify them.

13.2. Audience

This document has been created for incident response teams, system and network administrators, security staff, technical support staff, chief information security officers (CISOs), chief information officers (CIOs), computer security program managers, and others who are responsible for preparing for, or responding to, security incidents.

13.3. What is an event and incident?

Any change in the current state of a business process, service, system or infrastructure (hardware, software or people) that depends on the production environment. This change may include new servers, software, product development, or changes to the infrastructure of the IT network that supports them.

Changes in IT infrastructure may be required to respond to problems, external mandatory requirements such as: obligations arising from legislation, projects, upgrade initiatives or service improvement, and software development.

The change management process encompasses changes in systems and infrastructure in order to minimize errors and ensure that all changes are documented.

13.4. Categorization of an Incidents

We will normally have 4 types of incidents that can be handled by the incident and monitoring team, that can be;

- Critical
- High
- Medium
- Low

13.5. Incident Prioritization

According the 4 categories above, we can classify the priority of the incident and involve or handling correctly;

Category	Description
Critical (C)	- Environments are completely affected, and business impact are immediate
High (H)	- The damage caused by the Incident increases rapidly. - Work that cannot be completed by staff is highly time sensitive. - A minor Incident can be prevented from becoming a major Incident by acting immediately. - Several users with VIP status are affected.
Medium (M)	- The damage caused by the Incident increases considerably over time. - A single user with VIP status is affected.
Low (L)	- The damage caused by the Incident only marginally increases over time. - Work that cannot be completed by staff is not time sensitive.

Prioritizing the handling of the incident is perhaps the most critical decision point in the incident handling process. Incidents should not be handled on a first-come, first-served basis as a result of resource limitations. Instead, handling should be prioritized based on the relevant factors, such as the following:

- Functional Impact of the Incident. Incidents targeting IT systems typically impact the business functionality that those systems provide, resulting in some type of negative impact to the users of those systems. Incident handlers should consider how the incident will impact the existing functionality of the affected systems. Incident handlers should consider not only the current functional impact of the incident, but also the likely future functional impact of the incident if it is not immediately contained.

- Information Impact of the Incident. Incidents may affect the confidentiality, integrity, and availability of the organization's information. For example, a malicious agent may exfiltrate sensitive information. Incident handlers should consider how this information exfiltration will impact the organization's overall mission. An incident that results in the exfiltration of sensitive information may also affect other organizations if any of the data pertained to a partner organization.

- Recoverability from the Incident. The size of the incident and the type of resources it affects will determine the amount of time and resources that must be spent on recovering from that incident. In some instances, it is not possible to recover from an incident (e.g., if the confidentiality of sensitive information has been compromised) and it would not make sense to spend limited resources on an elongated incident handling cycle, unless that effort was directed at ensuring that a similar incident did not occur in the future. In other cases, an incident may require far more resources to handle than what an organization has available. Incident handlers should consider the effort necessary to actually recover from an incident and carefully weigh that against the value the recovery effort will create and any requirements related to incident handling.

13.6. Incident Impact

According to the criticality and impact of the incident the team will involve more or less people, put more or less focus and sometimes declare a situation that's need a war room to solve the problem. Another topic about war room will be in other topics.

Category	Description
Critical (c)	<ul><li>Business impact is immediate</li><li>Revenues impacts are high.</li></ul>
High (H)	<ul><li>A large number of staff are affected and/or not able to do their job.</li><li>A large number of customers are affected and/or acutely disadvantaged in some way.</li><li>The financial impact of the Incident is (for example) likely to exceed $10,000.</li><li>The damage to the reputation of the business is likely to be high.</li><li>Someone has been injured.</li></ul>
Medium (M)	<ul><li>A moderate number of staff are affected and/or not able to do their job properly.</li><li>A moderate number of customers are affected and/or inconvenienced in some way.</li></ul>

Low (L)	<ul><li>The financial impact of the Incident is (for example) likely to exceed $1,000 but will not be more than $10,000.</li><li>The damage to the reputation of the business is likely to be moderate.</li><li>A minimal number of staff are affected and/or able to deliver an acceptable service but this requires extra effort.</li><li>A minimal number of customers are affected and/or inconvenienced but not in a significant way.</li><li>The financial impact of the Incident is (for example) likely to be less than $1,000.</li><li>The damage to the reputation of the business is likely to be minimal.</li></ul>

13.7. Incident Priority Matrix

If classes are defined to rate urgency and impact (see above), an Urgency-Impact Matrix (also referred to as Incident Priority Matrix) can be used to define priority classes, identified in this example by colors and priority codes:

Level		Impact		
		H	M	N
Critical	H	1	2	3
	M	2	3	4
	L	3	4	5

13.8. Incident SLA

Following the table below you can find the documentation about the time for a group of priorities x criticality, the main thing to do is to verify in the committee if the numbers below can be achieved or can be supported by the business in the customer relationship.

Priority Code	Description	Target Response Time	Target Resolution Time
1	Critical	Immediate	1 Hour
2	High	10 Minutes	4 Hours
3	Medium	1 Hour	8 Hours
4	Low	4 Hours	24 Hours
5	Very low	1 Day	1 Week

14. Incident Management

Incident Management is a management process that handled and classify the priority and criticality of an incident, event or problem that happen in the production environment.

This approach ensures the standardized processes and methods are adopted to ensure efficiency and agility in all situations minimizing impacts to the business, services and systems.

Another point of approach used in the incident management is to be a bridge, during the crisis or incident, between the business and other strategic and technologic areas involved in the solution.

14.1. Objectives

The main objective of the Incident Management is to ensure that the incident is managed by a competent team, correctly recorded and subsequently evaluated to analyze the crisis and create a better process to prevent the problem happen again or other problems that's derivate of the problem continue to affect the business.

During a crisis normally, the employees lost the focus trying to protect yourselves than solving a high-level problem and prevent the problem happen again or the incident goes to a level that can't be managed.

15. Papers and Responsibility

15.1. Incident Management Manager

The Incident Manager is the most important person in the entire process and he is the driver of the situation following the standards or making sure the process is following all the steps and mainly to drive the committee. He is responsible and decide about all the communications that need to be done to the business area, actions that need to be executed and to determine if the incident can trigger a Disaster Recovery process and when the incident can be closed.

As a part of his activities, he must to categorize all incidents situations, changing the level if necessary and trigger the Incident Committee to discuss, record, solve, accept or reject a solution, and plan how to solve the incident and return the entire environment affected to the running state.

15.2. Incident Management Committee

The Incident Management Committee should be formed by all stakeholders of all the environment affected or involved directly or indirectly, including business and technology areas. The incident Committee is also responsible for evaluating the incident and declare a disaster recovery, when necessary, or initiate a War Room.

The Incident Committee shall meet when called upon by the Incident Manager to evaluate, prioritize, and plan the solution of a problem.

The evaluation of the requests should consider the risks to the business, financial implications and resources to correct the issue and solve the incident.

After solving the incident in the production environment and conducting post-incident evaluation to verify if the solution has been successfully implemented and without causing negative impacts on the environment, the committee must formally communicate all involved in the solution process all the points about the incident.

15.3. Emergency Committee (War Room)

The Emergency Committee should be created by the Incident Manager and the responsible that was included by the incident manager. This Committee is responsible for approving emergency modifications and can be connected with the Change Management Process including the Change Manager.

This Emergency committee have all the power, following the ethic and compliance lines to solve the problem using financial resources available or ability to change the architecture of one environment.

15.4. Committee Meeting

The committee can be created or called when a incident happen and the necessity to have a committee to solve the problem justify the situation.

15.5. Implementing Incident Management

The Incident Management Process implementation can follow the form created to be a "Guide", in a checklist format, during the implementation.

Checklist Implementation form was created to be the main point to follow during the process.

This form can be found in the Incident Management folder structure under the folder called "8. Checklist"

16. Incident Management Process

16.1. Incident Response Life Cycle

The image below shows a flow about the life cycle of an incident and how the incident can be managed in 4 steps. This is the simple way and no detailed process, but the entire 4 process goes deeply and more detailed.

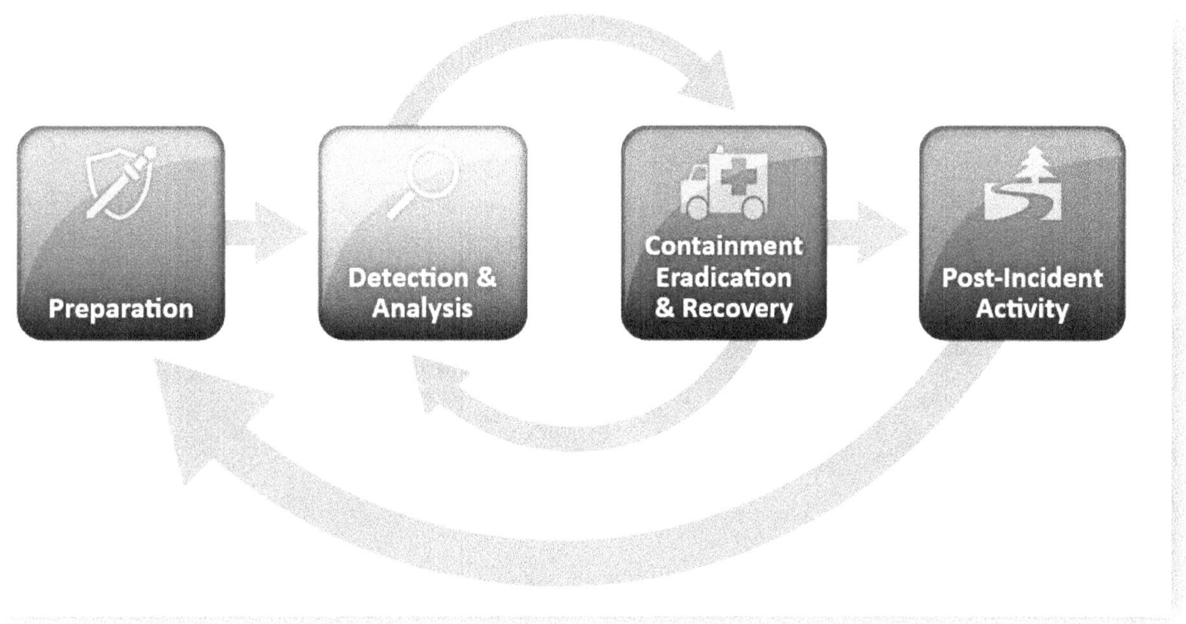

16.2. Diagraming and Flow

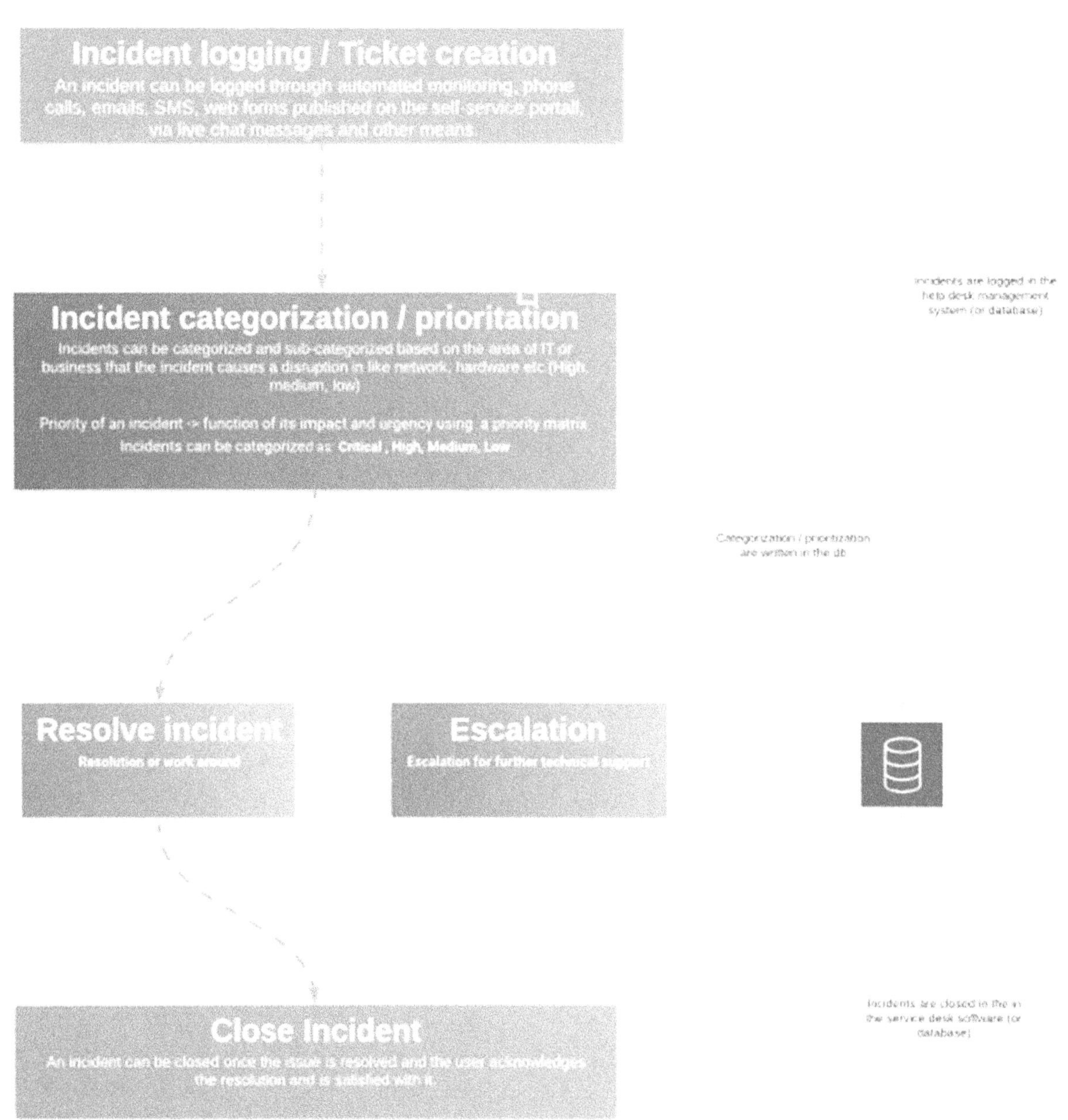

16.3. Preparing to Handle Incidents

The lists below provide examples of tools and resources available that may be of value during incident handling. These lists are intended to be a starting point for discussions about which tools and resources an organization's incident handlers need. For example, smartphones are one way to have resilient emergency communication and coordination mechanisms. An organization should have multiple (separate and different) communication and coordination mechanisms in case of failure of one mechanism.

Incident Handler Communications and Facilities:

- Contact information for team members and others within and outside the organization (primary and backup contacts), such as law enforcement and other incident response teams; information may include phone numbers, email addresses, public encryption keys (in accordance with the encryption software described below), and instructions for verifying the contact's identity.
- On-call information for other teams within the organization, including escalation information.
- Incident reporting mechanisms, such as phone numbers, email addresses, online forms, and secure instant messaging systems that users can use to report suspected incidents; at least one mechanism should permit people to report incidents anonymously.
- Issue tracking system for tracking incident information, status, etc.
- Smartphones to be carried by team members for off-hour support and onsite communications.
- Encryption software to be used for communications among team members, within the organization and with external parties.
- War room for central communication and coordination; if a permanent war room is not necessary or practical, the team should create a procedure for procuring a temporary war room when needed.
- Secure storage facility for securing evidence and other sensitive materials.

16.4. Incident Notification

When an incident is analyzed and prioritized, the incident response team needs to notify the appropriate individuals so that all who need to be involved will play their roles. Incident response policies should include provisions concerning incident reporting—at a minimum, what must be reported to whom and at what times (e.g., initial notification, regular status updates). The exact reporting requirements vary among organizations, but parties that are typically notified include:

- CIO
- Head of information security
- Local information security officer
- Other incident response teams within the organization
- External incident response teams (if appropriate)
- System owner
- Human resources (for cases involving employees, such as harassment through email)
- Public affairs (for incidents that may generate publicity)
- Legal department (for incidents with potential legal ramifications)
- Law enforcement (if appropriate)

During incident handling, the team may need to provide status updates to certain parties, even in some cases the entire organization. The team should plan and prepare several communication methods, including out-of-band methods (e.g., in person, paper), and select the methods that are appropriate for a particular incident.

Possible communication methods include:

- Email
- Website (internal, external or portal)
- Telephone calls.
- In person (e.g., daily briefings)
- Voice mailbox greeting (e.g., set up a separate voice mailbox for incident updates, and update the greeting message to reflect the current incident status; use the help desk's voice mail greeting)
- Paper (e.g., post notices on bulletin boards and doors, hand out notices at all entrance points).

16.5. Registry the incident

The registration of the incident is a very important task and will give to us an idea and a historical record about all the incidents that's happen and how was the work team to fix and what is the solution used.

Below you can find a Table that inform the name convention that must be used to identify the excel file that will receive all the information's about the incident.

Unique Identifier of the Incident
INC_YYYYMMDD-XXX
<ul><li>INC – Incident Identification</li><li>YYYYMMDD – Date of the Change Request</li><li>XXX – Sequential Number (started by 001 until 999)</li></ul>

1. Revision post-implementation and closure

After Implementation and Testing, the Change Committee shall review the change with the requestor to determine whether the implementation has been successful, allowing the achievement of the expected objectives or not.

Once approved, the record of the change must be terminated. The associated procedures and manuals must be updated as needed.

2. Closure and Registering

As soon the post-implementation was done and all the documentation was approved the Incident Manager must to save all the information in a safety storage, communicate to all the involved that the case/incident are closed and catalog the incident in the right place (see attachments descriptions in the topic below).

17. Change Management Process

17.1. Presentation

Experience has shown that IT incidents that normally affect the business are associated with uncontrolled changes. The causes of these incidents are numerous and may include lack of resources, insufficient planning, no testing or problems in the early stages of change.

Change Management aims to ensure that standardized methods and processes are applied to all changes in the IT environment. This approach allows changes to be a) reviewed and tested, b) evaluated for the impact of their implementation and c) supported by a plan to return to the previous state of the IT environment in case of failures after implementation.

This process significantly reduces the number and impact of incidents caused by changes, such as unavailability of IT services, and maintains the balance between the need for change and the adverse impacts of its implementation.

The next pages of this document describe the key aspects of the Change Management process covering your request and the follow-up phase after implementation.

17.2. What is a Change?

Any change in the current state of a business process, service, system or infrastructure (hardware, software or people) that depends on the production environment. This change may include new servers, software, product development, or changes to the infrastructure of the IT network that supports them.

Changes in IT infrastructure may be required to respond to problems, external mandatory requirements such as: obligations arising from legislation, projects, upgrade initiatives or service improvement, and software development.

The change management process encompasses changes in systems and infrastructure in order to minimize errors and ensure that all changes are documented.

17.3. Change Management and Agile

The Change Management process and the Agile process, as discussed in the opening chapters of the book, can and should coexist very harmoniously.

But for this process to be harmonious, it is very important that there is synchronism between the change approval process and the spring creation process.

We should not discuss here how this process should happen but make it clear that a change should not happen in production without the approval of a committee.

17.4. Harmonic existence

As a mantra technology manager must daily sing together so that the universal vibrations help in this harmonious coexistence.

We can also create a to-do or step-by-step list that will help and avoid the horrible scene of two technology managers singing a mantra in the office.

- **Sprints** can only be created with the base documents of changes that will occur in production.
- **Since** all documents are already loaded with information about items that will go into production, I suggest that at the time of sprint creation the sprint should be sent to the change management committee for prior approval.
- **It is** always known that a sprint may not have all the items that were in the artifacts that make up a documentation, so the committee should create a rule for these cases.
- **The approval** committee should always consider the agile process and make some concessions and be a little flexible.

I assure everyone involved in the change management process that if these above are followed the change management process with Agile will always be a success story.

17.5. Change Management Types?

We will normally have 2 types of changes made and will be submitted to the change committee for approval;

Normal – normal changes are those that were created following the rules of the committee respecting the date of submission of the change and the dates and times of execution.

Emergency - are those changes that did not follow the correct flow because they needed to be implemented in an emergency to reestablish an environment that is stopped, unstable or to meet a legal determination that does not allow to wait for the normal process.

Even the change being emergency it must follow some rules, regardless of how critical or emergency it is according to data below;

- the form must be filled out with all fields mainly those on data on how the current environment is being preserved, such as backup or return process in case of failure

- presentation of successful test evidence

- presentation, on the form, of a clear rollback process and which respects the existing infrastructure and rules of the area.

- approval of at least 2 committee members must be approved or formalized

17.6. What is a Change Management?

Change Management is a change management process that includes changes in the business environment, services and systems.

This approach ensures that standardized processes and methods are adopted to ensure efficiency and agility in all changes minimizing impacts on the IT environment and risks to the business, services and systems arising from changes implemented in an uncontrolled way.

18. Objectives

Ensure that the change is recorded and subsequently evaluated, authorized, prioritized, planned, tested, implemented, documented and analyzed in a controlled manner.

19. Papers and Responsibility

19.1. Change Management Manager

The Change Manager is responsible for the change management process and must categorize all change requests and trigger the Change Committee to discuss, approve, reject and plan implementation of the requested changes.

19.2. Change Management Committee

The Change Committee should be formed by all stakeholders of change, including business and technology areas. The Change Committee is also responsible for evaluating the request for changes and scheduling the date and time for its implementation.

The Change Committee shall meet when called upon by the Change Manager to evaluate, prioritize, and plan the implementation of the requested changes. The evaluation of requests should consider the risks to the business, financial implications and resources to implement the change.

After implementing the change in the production environment and conducting post-implementation evaluation to verify that the change has been successfully implemented and without causing negative impacts on the environment, the committee must be communicated and the change record must be terminated.

19.3. Emergencial Committee

The Emergency Committee should be formed by the Change Manager and the Manager responsible for the change. This Committee is responsible for approving Emergency change requests.

19.4. Execution Team

The IT (administration, development, infrastructure and operations) area is responsible for implementing the change and ensuring that it is completed in accordance with the implementation plan. If the change is not successful, the executing area is responsible for implementing the return plan.

19.5. Committee Meeting

The committee must determine a day and time for the meeting to take place in accordance with a schedule and periodicity.

This meeting must be balanced with the submission limits of the changes to ensure that the areas that need the change are able to be submitted and evaluated.

20. Rules and definitions

All the rules about the entire change management process will be defined in the first meeting that the committee program. The guide to help the group to achieve each step is the form called "Implementation Checklist" that must be used.

In this meeting the form, called "RFC Definitions", must be filled, saved in a safety place and published to the group to make sure that everyone involved in the process understand the rules.

21. Scope and exceptions

This policy applies to all changes related to the infrastructure (servers, networks, firewalls, etc.) and Systems (applications, database, operating systems, etc.) provided by the company.

Changes related to infrastructure / non-productive systems (development environment and testing) are outside the scope of the policy.

Any exception to this policy must have a written approval, a business justification, the risks assumed and the compensatory controls, if applicable, must be documented.

22. Change Management Process

22.1. Implementing CMP

The Change Management Process or CMP implementation can follow the form created to be a "Guide" during the implementation.

Checklist Implementation form was created to be the main point to follow during the process, associated a this form the implementation team can use another form called "RFC Definitions" where they save the definitions asked during the checklist and use the file to publishing the rules and informations.

22.2. Change Management

The Change Management process must ensure that changes are reviewed, authorized, tested, approved and implemented so that each step is monitored. Changes related to infrastructure and systems will be managed and implemented in accordance with the change process, which should contain the following steps:

22.3. Sending and Registering the change request

The change process begins with the submission of the completed change request form. The form must be completed with the change applicant's information, description and reason for the change, description of the risk of not implementing the change and the dependencies involved (where applicable). Once completed, it should be sent to <*rfc@example.com*> for the request to be evaluated at the next meeting of the Committee.

The emergency changes must be identified in the request form and in the title of the sending e-mail of the form with the text **"Request for Emergency Change"**. In the case of emergency changes, requests must be sent directly to <*rfc@example.com*>.

22.4. Acceptance and revision

Upon receipt and review by the Quality Reviewer and Change Manager, the change shall receive a unique identification number, which shall be generated as described below. Then the change should be sent to the Change Committee for discussion.

22.5. Freezing Period

In order to keep the environment safe and stable, the committee must create, disclose and follow a table with dates and periods of the year (determined with beginning, middle and end) that may affect the changes or even prevent them.

These periods usually coincide with periods of the year where there are parties, collective holidays or critical processes that need to be performed for legal reasons or force of law.

It should have a table with 4 types of freezes according to the example below;

Normal - Only when the RFC was submitted to the committee.

Medium - Only when the RFC has been submitted to the committee and is a change that affects something that needs to be corrected to ensure the operation of the business or for a legal reason.

Critical - Only emergency changes are submitted to the committee that will ensure that a stopping environment returns to work or for legal reasons.

Blocked - Completely blocked from submitting or applying RFC unless it is something emergency.

Unique Identifier of the Change
RFCDDMMAAAAXXX
<ul><li>RFC – Acronym for Request for Change</li><li>DDMMAAAA – Date of the Change Request</li><li>XXX – Sequential Number (started by 001 until 999)</li></ul>

22.6. Discussion and Prioritization

The Change Committee should discuss, evaluate and prioritize changes. In the discussion should be evaluated the risks to the business originated from the implementation, resources required and implementation windows available for implementation. The committee's discussion and decisions must be recorded in the minutes and in the Change Control.

A change should not be directed to implementation in case of absence of key person for discussion in the Change Committee. In this situation, the change must be resubmitted for discussion at the next committee meeting.

22.7. Development, test, implementation and rollback plan

Whenever possible, the change must be developed and tested in a virtual environment segregated from the production environment to avoid impacts on business processes during the testing phase.

The testing phase should include the Return Plan test to ensure that the Services and Systems can be reestablished from failures or instabilities in the production environment after the change implementation.

In case of negative results after the tests, the change should not be implemented and should return to the development process or alternative solution should be defined.

The implementation must be carried out according to the agreed implementation window, after implementation the change must be tested by the applicant.

22.8. Revision post-implementation and closure

After Implementation and Testing, the Change Committee shall review the change with the requestor to determine whether the implementation has been successful, allowing the achievement of the expected objectives or not.

Once approved, the record of the change must be terminated. The associated procedures and manuals must be updated as needed.

23. References

1. Gallacher, Ian, et al. "ITIL Foundation Essentials: The Exam Facts You Need." IT Governance Ltd, 2012.
2. Van Haren Publishing. "ITIL Foundation Handbook: Pocketbook from the Official Publisher of ITIL." Van Haren Publishing, 2018.
3. OGC (Office of Government Commerce). "ITIL Service Strategy." The Stationery Office, 2011.
4. OGC (Office of Government Commerce). "ITIL Service Design." The Stationery Office, 2011.
5. OGC (Office of Government Commerce). "ITIL Service Transition." The Stationery Office, 2011.
6. OGC (Office of Government Commerce). "ITIL Service Operation." The Stationery Office, 2011.
7. OGC (Office of Government Commerce). "ITIL Continual Service Improvement." The Stationery Office, 2011.
8. Van Haren Publishing. "ITIL Lifecycle Publication Suite (5 books)." Van Haren Publishing, 2011.
9. Vernon Lloyd. "Implementing ITIL Change and Release Management." Van Haren Publishing, 2008.
10. Liz Gallacher and Helen Morris. "ITIL Foundation Exam Study Guide." John Wiley & Sons, 2012.
11. ITIL references - https://wiki.en.it-processmaps.com/index.php/Main_Page
12. Incident Response by NIST – https://nist.gov